LOVE, LIFE *and* LONELINESS

David F. Noah

iUniverse, Inc.
New York Bloomington

LOVE, LIFE and LONELINESS

iUniverse books may be ordered through booksellers or by contacting:

iUniverse
1663 Liberty Drive
Bloomington, IN 47403
www.iuniverse.com
1-800-Authors (1-800-288-4677)

ISBN: 978-1-4401-1894-4 (pbk)
ISBN: 978-1-4401-1895-1 (ebk)

Printed in the United States of America
iUniverse rev. date: 2/27/09

Foreward

Poetry is inarguably a passionate art form. For centuries it has provided us with an outlet for exploring our innermost thoughts and emotions. Regardless of the style or subject chosen, we are able to express our intimate feelings using this ancient tradition. Poetry allows us to communicate issues that we might not be able to otherwise openly discuss. It affords us the opportunity to reevaluate ourselves, our relationships with others, our station in life, and the world around us. Poetry can be therapeutic, allowing us to work through issues in our lives to find solutions, clarity, comfort, and peace of mind.

This book is a compilation of my work and some of my favorite poems by some very talented people. (The poems written by other authors have their names after their work. All other poems are written by the book's author.) We all look at life from different angles and points of view. Through the course of one's life, we come upon many trials and tribulations. What defines our true being is how we deal, learn and come away from these situations. Much of my writing is either life experiences or feelings I have had in my life. I try to write in a manner that puts someone in my place and lets them feel and sense the emotions of the moment.

Acknowledgements

Monna Innominata (I loved you first)
Monna Innominata (I wish I could remember)
Remember

all by Christina Rossetti

The three works by Christina Rossetti used in this book were found at Poets.Org.

How Do I Love Thee

by Elizabeth Barrett Browning

The work by Elizabeth Barrett Browning used in this book was found at Poets.Org.

If

by Rudyard Kipling

The work by Rudyard Kipling used in this book was found at Poets.Org.

In Memoriam A.H.H. XXVII

by Lord Alfred Tennyson

The work by Lord Alfred Tennyson used in this book was found at Poets.Org.

CONTENTS

Love

Love

Love is like the taste of sweet pastries fresh from the oven.
Love is like the smell of Spring showers in a meadow of flowers.

Love is watching playful puppies romp without a care in the world.
Love is hearing the laughter and voices of children at play.

Love is having a pit in your stomach every time you think of a special person.
Love is an aching to be near that special someone when they are far away.

Love is a sense of oneness with another who makes you whole.
Love is a feeling, a sight, a smell and a taste of everything wonderful.

Someone New

When you meet someone for the very first time,
Your defenses go up, bells and whistles will chime.
We look to our past and recall all those stories,
We try not to notice their fame or their glory.

We try to keep our emotions intact,
When all we can do is barely hold back.
They smile and greet us and talk for an hour,
They smell so good with the scent of a flower.

We are dazed and confused, could this really be,
There really is someone who honestly likes me.
We relax once more and let our guard down,
Well here we go again, it's another go round.

The first kiss is so wonderful, the next is unreal,
"Could this be heaven", I'm beginning to feel.
With visions of grandeur, our hearts start to leap,
When all of a sudden, I awake from my sleep.

Was this just a dream, or was it for real,
The sounds, the emotions, how can I deal.
I know what I heard and I saw with my eye,
For this to be imagined, would just make me cry.

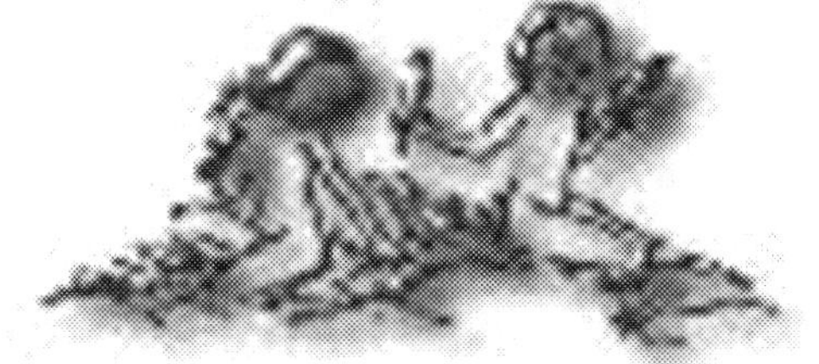

Monna Innominata

(I loved you first)

I loved you first: but afterwards your love,
Outsoaring mine, sang such a loftier song
As drowned the friendly cooings of my dove.
Which owes the other most? My love was long,
And yours one moment seemed to wax more strong;
I loved and guessed at you, you construed me
And loved me for what might or might not be-
Nay, weights and measures do us both a wrong.
For verily love knows not 'mine' or 'thine';
With separate 'I' and 'thou' free love has done,
For one is both and both are one in love:
Rich love knows nought of 'thine that is not mine';
Both have the strength and both the length thereof,
Both of us, of the love which makes us one.

By Christina Rossetti

To Love Someone

To love someone with all your heart,
Is a challenge, it's a risk and maybe not smart.
But the rewards are passion and love for a few,
It is well worth the gamble; it's all up to you.

The First Date

Your stomach is tied in knots,
Your heart beats are heavy.
Your throat has a bolder,
That would hold a large levy.

Your skin is all clammy,
Your temperature begins to rise.
Perspiration begins to flow,
Is this dating thing wise?

The brain starts to short circuit,
You are tongue tied and choke.
Your hands all have thumbs,
You swear you smell smoke.

This thing they call dating,
Let me make this so clear.
There are two of you shaking,
And fretting with fear.

Relax and be yourself,
Take one step, then the next,
Remember, who you are with,
They aren't a witch with a hex.

Have fun, enjoy the night,
This is someone you want to know.
Let the time be your guide,
And let a Friendship begin to grow.

The Loves of Ones' Life

In the world of Love, there are many different kinds,
From all different countries, from all different minds.
From Puppy Love and childhood crushes, to total admiration,
To the Love of one's country, to the Love of our Nation.

There is the Love of one's self, so selfish and bare,
There's the Love of a lifetime which is genuinely rare.
There's the Love of a friend, so faithful and true,
Who'll protect you from others, who'll protect you from you.

There's the Love of a companion, who loves to make you giggle,
They hold you and woo you and make your insides jiggle.
They can play your body like a fine wine of the past,
They can melt your heart slowly and make your pulse fast.

With the lick of a toe, or the stroke of the hair,
You can send one the feelings of a world free of care.
With the stroke of a thigh or the touch of the back,
You make one so care free, their senses they lack.

When coupled in passion, all worlds seem to crash,
With reckless abandon our walls we do smash.
We all do our best, our partners to please,
Our goal is pure ecstasy, our bodies we squeeze.

Love is the giving, the whole of one's self,
Without caring for a person's status or wealth.
To give to another the depths of your heart,
Means you'll always be together, never apart.

Remember the good, the better and the best,
Make room for the memories and treasure the rest.
The Loves of one's life, so treasured and dear,
Should be kept in our thoughts and always be near.

How Do I Love Thee?

How do I love thee? Let me count the ways.
I love thee to the depth and breadth and height
My soul can reach, when feeling out of sight
For the ends of being and ideal grace.
I love thee to the level of every day's
Most quiet need, by sun and candle-light.
I love thee freely, as men strive for right.
I love thee purely, as they run from praise.
I love thee with the passion put to use
In my old griefs, and with my childhood's faith.
I love thee with a love I seemed to lose
With my lost saints. I love thee with the breath,
Smiles, tears, of all my life; and if God choose,
I shall but love thee better after death.

By Elizabeth Barrett Browning

YOU & I

I Love your laugh,
I Love your smile.
I've only known you,
A short, short while.

You make me feel silly,
Like a giddy school kid.
Whenever I'm with you,
My inhibitions I rid.

You make me laugh,
You make me smile.
You make our time together,
So very much worth while.

I know how I feel,
I hope you do to!
Now and forever,
I'LL ALWAYS LOVE YOU!

Moonlight Encounter

As the waves gently crash upon the shore,
The heavenly sunset begins to fade away.
Emotions begin to swell and grow within us,
And we know, everything is right.

The full moon begins to rise and glow brightly in the sky,
We walk, hand in hand along the shore.
Our feet, wading in the surf, the tide rushing in and out.
The sand falling between our toes like an hourglass.

We stop, we embrace, a slow passionate kiss.
Our bodies silhouetted by the ambiance of the moon.
A gentle breeze begins to blow, surrounding our bodies.
Sending chills and tingles of delight through our senses.

We hold each other tightly, as if there is no tomorrow.
Neither of us moving, not wanting to disturb the silence.
Then, when time seems to have stopped and all is quiet.
Those mystical words are heard, “I Love You”.

Marriage

When two people meet for the very first time,
They are giddy and bashful and their faces just shine.
They talk and they laugh, their hearts all a glow,
Like two little school kids on a date at the show.

First one date, then two, then you ask me to stay,
I pause for a second, then I say "Well OK".
A friendship has started, a relationship too,
What started as one, has quickly become two.

Our money we pool, what there is isn't much,
We scrimp and we save, we can't afford to go Dutch.
To speak of a wedding this soon would be crazy,
But just call me nuts, you've made my world hazy.

My feelings I hide, they're buried so deep,
You want but the truth, this promise I'll keep.
You asked so I'll tell you, a lie I can't tell,
The truth from my lips, you know me so well.

We know this is right, something precious and true,
A wedding on the horizon, it's for me and for you.
The day was in May, back in nineteen ninety-two,
That wonderful time when you said, "Yes, I Do".

We've all had our struggles, our tiffs and our spats,
Thank God it never came to throwing rocks or using bats.
The years have been good to us, it's so plain to see,
Our health, wealth and happiness abundant they be.

So what of our vows, we are saying here today,
To love, honor and cherish and then there's obey.
For richer or poorer, in sickness and in health,
Please no more sickness, my favorite is wealth.

I can't promise diamonds, emeralds or jewels,
I can't promise horses or clown dancing fools.
What I give, I give freely and straight from the heart,
Please no beans and weenies, the gas makes me fart.

All kidding aside, this is straight from the heart,
You are the love of my life, so beautiful and smart.
So here are those words you all want to hear,
I'll speak them with grace, but don't shed a tear.

But here we are now, fifteen long and dismal years later,
We are back where we started, far richer and greater.
So will I or won't I say those words that once was,
Well here goes another fifteen, "OK, yes I does"!

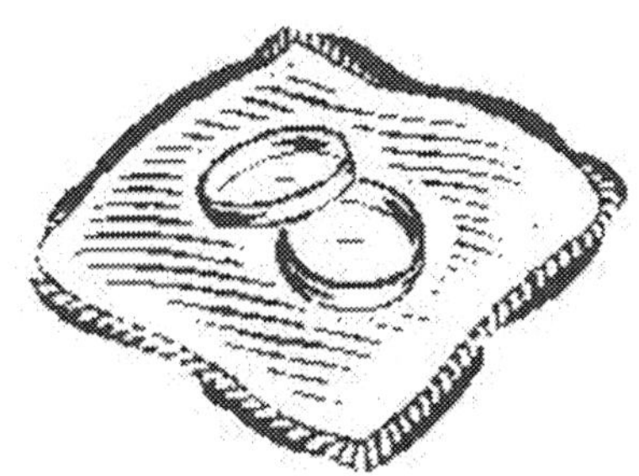

A Gentle Caress

We lay together like two spoons in a drawer,
Our bodies entwined, engulfed in the moment.
The tumultuous storm exploded outside,
Her body shook with every crack of thunder.
I nuzzled my face in the back of her neck,
I whispered in her ear that all would be OK.

She sighed a low moan as she backed into my arms,
I gently caressed her arm as she cooed in approval.
Rain ravaged the house for what seemed like hours,
Lightning illuminated our bodies in flashes of pleasure.
My arms wrapped tightly around her shuddering body,
With each kiss of her neck, her toes began to curl.

We face each other, embrace and begin to kiss,
The passion and yearning begins to swell within.
The flood waters rise with the pounding rain,
The climate begins to rise and our skin dampens.
As we regain our senses, our bodies begin to relax,
I'm not sure where the storm was stronger, inside or out.

Life

Life

In our Life, each of us has choices of the path that we will take.
With our first step our destiny is laid out for us to walk.
What we decide with each new step will determine our new path.
Step by step our lives are changed by each new decision.

Whether I turn left or right, my life will change for better or worse.
Each decision can have multiple out comes and different paths.
For what we choose will not only effect our lives, but those around us.
Our lives intertwine those around us and can change our lives forever.

A Chance Of A Lifetime

In every one's life, there comes such a time,
When the clouds move away and the planets align.
Where sadness once lived, a joy starts to flow,
Where darkness and gloom were, a heart starts to grow.

Since sadness and pain, my companions had been,
No joy or laughter my soul had within.
The despair and anguish my life had lived for,
Was turning to ashes, to return never more.

A chance of a lifetime, a moment in life,
When gloom turned to smiles and eliminated strife.
The laughter and joy that once had been gone,
Is filling my heart, since nothing is wrong.

To meet someone wonderful, so beautiful and true,
Who took away the sadness and made the skies blue.
Could this be the answer, could this be the one,
Is love on the horizon, is the sadness all done.

The joy that I feel in the depths of my soul,
Has got to be real, I'm not playing a role.
This chance of a lifetime, I must hold on to,
It comes along but once, it can happen to you.

A New Day

We wake up every morning,
Hoping this won't be our last.
We thank the Lord for each new day,
And his blessings of the past.

We go to school each day at dawn,
The lessons for to learn.
We rack our brain and study hard,
A degree we plan to earn.

We work our fingers to the bone,
Each day from nine to five.
We try to save each dime we can,
To survive and stay alive.

We raise our children every day,
Their futures we hope to set.
They find a mate and settle down,
Their family hasn't started yet.

We age with grace as time goes by,
So beautiful for a few
The cycle of life goes on and on,
This saga must start anew.

Patience

Patience is a virtue, a talent and a chore,
The more we try to learn, the more we must explore.
Whenever life throws us, a lesson or a curve,
We all do our best, to avoid or to swerve.

No matter what path we choose to endure,
We plant our feet firmly and try to be sure.
The decisions we make, from large ones to small,
Will decide our fate in life, it will affect us one and all.

Whenever we decide the path we will take,
The life we select, our destiny we make.
The world will afford us the chance to succeed,
It will open its' arms for whatever our needs.

Be wise, be truthful and be ready for strife,
Be prepared to make decisions the rest of your life.
A plan for the future will help you succeed,
But patience is the answer, it is what we all need.

Friends

In each of our lives, we meet many souls,
From all walks of life, playing many different roles.
Some we care for, no matter their walk in life,
Others we shun, for their battles and strife.

There are some we meet, we love and adore,
As we learn of their lives, we want even more.
They touch our soul and make our hearts yearn,
The more they give, the more we want to learn.

Others we meet, merely show us disdain,
To this kind of people, we try to refrain.
Possessions and gain are what they search for,
No matter what we give, they only want more.

The best kind of people, are those who want not,
No matter their trouble, they love what they've got.
In getting to know them, we find the truest of things,
Their passion for life, is the best that life brings.

As we gain their respect and learn of their kin,
We open ourselves up and let their lives in.
These are the truest, the noblest, the best,
These are our friends, to hell with the rest.

If

If you can keep you head when all about you
Are losing theirs and blaming it on you;
If you can trust yourself when all men doubt you,
But make allowance for their doubting too;
If you can wait and not be tired by waiting,
Or, being lied about, don't deal in lies,
Or, being hated, don't give way to hating,
And yet don't look too good, nor talk to wise;

If you can dream – and not make dreams your master;
If you can think – and not make thoughts your aim;
If you can meet with triumph and disaster
And treat those two impostors just the same;
If you can bear to hear the truth you've spoken
Twisted by knaves to make a trap for fools,
Or watch the things you gave life to broken,
And stoop and build'em up with worn out tools;

If you can make one heap of all your winnings
And risk it on one turn of pitch-and-toss,
And lose, and start again at your beginnings
And never breathe a word about your loss;
If you can force your heart and nerve and sinew
To serve your turn long after they are gone,
And so hold on when there is nothing in you
Except the Will which says to them: "Hold on";

If you can talk with crowds and keep your virtue,
Or walk with kings – nor lose the common touch;
If neither foes nor loving friends can hurt you;
If all men count with you, but none too much;
If you can fill the unforgiving minute
With sixty seconds' worth of distance run –
Yours is the Earth and everything that's in it,
And – which is more – you'll be a Man, my son!

By Rudyard Kipling

Children

Children are a blessing, a joy and a curse,
You give all you've got, with no bottomless purse.
They scream and they cry, they don't mind at all,
But you love them and teach them, you give them your all.

From diapers to grade school, your there when they need,
For guidance and patience are all that we plead.
From high school on up, we hope they have grown,
We've given them the tools to be out on their own.

Now our children have children, who need the same care,
We hope we have taught them what they must beware.
Our children are our hopes, our dreams and our lives,
Be proud, be honest, and everyone will survive.

Pets

They come into our lives to bring happiness and joy,
Their love is unconditional, our hearts they employ.
They protect us and guard us from danger when near,
They give of themselves, never bending to fear.

They play, they romp, they shred your favorite shoes,
They run around the yard, your treasures they lose.
With hugs and kisses, their affections they bestow,
They lay at our feet, not a care do they know.

From Madam and Shadow, these girls were so gifted,
To Cleo and Lacey, from our laps must be lifted.
Then there's Hootie and Gabby, now that's a cool pair,
These are my family, my children, so rare.

Their temperament is gentle, so calming and pure,
They help keep us healthy, our emotions will endure.
To love them and care for them is all that they ask,
They're our best friends forever, their memories will last.

An Angel

One day I found an Angel,
Who took me by the hand.
She led me down the path of life,
The journey was oh so grand.

This Angel had a heart of gold,
Her grace and touch so pure.
She granted me her gift of love,
A treasure that will endure.

My Angel stays right by my side,
Her patience is from above.
I'm nothing without my Angel,
Nothing without her Love.

Hawaii

Blue skies,
Fresh air,
Land of enchantment,
Land without care.

Tropical forests,
Snorkeling and diving,
Hula and Luau's,
There's no need for driving.

Clear water,
Large fish,
Beautiful women,
Make a wish.

Huge waves,
Volcanoes to,
Can't wait to go back,
How about you?

Loneliness

Loneliness

In a crowded room, with people we all may know,
A person can feel completely isolated, estranged by all.
Without a loved one, without a friend to turn to,
Loneliness seems to be our only feeling, our worst enemy.

There are times we can stand before a crowd and not see a sole,
Amidst the people who say they care for us, we are told.
We see their bodies, but they seem to have no connection,
The Loneliness we feel cannot be described, it's only pain.

When your heart is heavy and your mind starts to race,
There's a feeling of being stranded, a sense of being alone.
You start to imagine the world has passed you by,
For Loneliness seems to be your closest companion.

To be separated from your loved ones, to be far from home,
Can leave your heart with a hole, to large to climb from.
The ache sinks to the depths and the pit of your soul,
With Loneliness, the only cure is true friends and loved ones.

FEAR

Fear is an emotion we all can't afford,
When someone's in trouble, we love and adore.
To feel helpless and useless to aid and abet,
To free them from danger we'll never forget.

You feel lonely and isolated, unable to act,
You want for their safety, their soul still intact.
You worry and stress, wondering which way to turn,
Your patience and energy continue to burn.

The fear of unknowing is the greatest of all,
The more we try to conquer it, the further we fall.
The harder we try to overcome our fears.
Puts wrinkles on your face and adds nothing but years.

Monna Innominata
(I wish I could remember)

I wish I could remember that first day,
First hour, first moment of your meeting me,
If bright or dim the season, it might be
Summer or Winter for aught I can say;
So unrecorded did it slip away,
So blind was I to see and to foresee,
So dull to mark the budding of my tree
That would not blossom for many a May.
If only I could recollect it, such
A day of days! I let it come and go
As traceless as a thaw of bygone snow;
It seemed to mean so little, meant so much;
If only now I could recall that touch,
First touch of hand in hand – Did one but know!

By Christina Rossetti

Lonely

Have you ever felt lonely?
Have you ever been sad?
Does life make you frustrated?
Don't you want to get mad?

Have you ever felt unloved?
Secluded by all the rest.
Have you ever felt put down?
When you know you did your best.

Do you ever want to run and hide?
Do you close yourself in?
Does the world look so big and mean?
Is this a battle you can't win?

People can be so heartless.
They can really be so cruel.
They rate our lives to their own scale.
They feed our rage with fuel.

When you think life has passed you by,
And no one seems to care.
Just close your eyes and dream of Heaven,
For life really does begin there!

Scared

A shadow or sound, make your hairs stand on end,
Your skin feels all clammy, your knees begin to bend.
Your hands begin to shake and feet must weigh a ton,
You look around both left and right for a way to run.

Your heart beats pound like a hammer upon a nail,
Your chest starts to tighten and you start feeling ill.
Your body tenses as if it were pinned inside a vice,
Your mind begins to wander and you start to think twice.

So what am I afraid of, what is it that I don't see?
This thing they call love, has really started to affect me.
The fact of not knowing, wondering what she will say,
Keeps me dazed and confused for most of the day.

The absence of knowledge has thrown me for a spin,
When I stop and think logically, I think I might win.
To be scared of the unknown without knowing why,
Will stop you from living and giving your best try.

ANGER

Anger is an emotion best kept deep inside,
When it lifts its fiery head, everything must hide.
Can it be controlled or is it in a rage,
For those unwilling to try, they are kept in a cage.

Anger can be positive or the cause is destruction,
Without strength and will, there is no production.
The rage that swells deep inside of our soul,
Should be harnessed and tethered to help reach our goal.

The best way to keep all the rage deep inside,
Is to bear all your feelings, have nothing to hide.
Be as honest and sincere with everyone you meet,
And don't be afraid, to say "HI" when you greet.

Remember

Remember me when I am gone away,
Gone far away into the silent land;
When you can no more hold me by the hand,
Nor I half turn to go yet turning stay.
Remember me when no more day by day
You tell me of our future that you planned:
Only remember me; you understand
It will be late to counsel then or pray.
Yet if you should forget me for a while
And afterwards remember, do not grieve:
For if the darkness and corruption leave
A vestige of the thoughts that once I had,
Better by far you should forget and smile
Than that you should remember and be sad.

By Christina Rossetti

LOSS

The loss of a loved one, so close and so dear,
Is the reason for panic, it's the reason for fear.
We dare to hang on with the strength of an Ape,
We cling to their memories like a vine to a grape.

We cherish our family, our friends and the few,
We mourn their passing as the loved ones we knew.
Whenever life's path seems to put us on hold,
We cinch up our belts and we try to be bold.

We try to live our lives the best that we can,
We hope that our memory will benefit man.
The loss of a loved one, will be painful to endure,
But our lives will be richer, for this I am sure.

Leaving

To leave someone that you truly love,
Takes a power and strength sent from up above.
Whatever the problem, whoever is to blame,
You can't go on in love if there isn't a flame.

To turn around and walk away,
To know they want you to stop and stay.
Your heart skips a beat and you want to cry,
It leaves you shattered and you're not sure why.

You love someone, yet you have to go,
You want to stay, but they say no.
You're really not sure which way to turn,
You only know you're going to crash and burn.

This person you love, you know you will miss,
You'll be deprived of their hug; you'll yearn for their kiss.
The person, the love, has all gone a wry,
And there you are, all hung out to dry.

You turn, one last time, with a quick little glance,
In hopes of a miracle or at least one last chance.
But the door has been closed; it's locked up tight,
No matter your will, you haven't got the might.

Is leaving the answer, do I have another choice,
I weigh all of my options, I search for your voice.
If I stay it will be OK, if I leave I'll have to pay,
But leaving's not an option, it is the only way,

Decisions

As you turn each corner in this game we call life,
There are decisions we make, like a job or a wife.
How we deal with these choices along the way,
Defines who we are and how we grow each day.

From cradle to grave we encounter many things,
You're never really sure what the next turn may bring.
Prosperity or being destitute are paths that can be,
The choice you decide, determine the wealth you see.

The beauty of decisions, is there's no right or wrong,
Each path that we take leads us where we belong.
Our life has a destiny that's predetermined at birth,
We get to select the path that determines its worth.

Remember to choose wisely; to err can cause pain,
Every path that you pick may alter what will remain.
Whatever you decide with each step along your path,
That makes you who you are, you do the math.

In Memoriam A. H. H.
1833 – 1849 (1850)

XXVII

I envy not in any moods
The captive void of noble rage,
The linnet born within the cage,
That never knew the summer woods:

I envy not the beast that takes
His license in the field of time,
Unfetter'd by the sense of crime,
To whom a conscience never wakes;

Nor, what may count itself as blest,
The heart that never plighted troth
But stagnates in the weeds of sloth;
Nor any want-begotten rest.

I hold it true, whate'er befall;
I feel it, I sorrow most;
'Tis better to have loved and lost
Than never to have loved at all.

By Lord Alfred Tennyson

In each of our lives, we encounter many unique situations that help us determine who and what we are to become in life. The emotions and feelings we all have are what mold our personalities. I have created this work using my own experiences and emotions. I have traveled throughout the world and met many amazing people in my journeys. My life has been a roller coaster going from an athlete to an entrepreneur, to serving in the military and even working for the Federal Government. I live in the mid-west and enjoy the laid back style of small town living. I enjoy meeting people and hearing about their life and the journeys they have taken.

Love, Life and Loneliness is a book of Poetry that walks us through life's lessons and hopefully it will help your emotions as you grow in life.